THE PHASES OF MATTER

CHEMISTRY BOOK GRADE 1
CHILDREN'S CHEMISTRY BOOKS

Speedy Publishing LLC
40 E. Main St. #1156
Newark, DE 19711
www.speedypublishing.com

Copyright © 2017

All Rights reserved. No part of this book may be reproduced or used in any way or form or by any means whether electronic or mechanical, this means that you cannot record or photocopy any material ideas or tips that are provided in this book

Everything around you is considered matter. Molecules and atoms are composed of matter. Anything that takes up space and has mass is considered matter. To put it in more simple terms, the amount of stuff in any object is considered its mass.

Even though we find matter all over our Universe, it can be found only in very few forms on planet Earth.

Read further to learn about the different phases of matter in chemistry, as well as how they can get from one phase to another.

Plasma

FIVE STATES OF MATTER

These are known as Plasmas, Gases, Liquids, Solids, and the Bose-Einstein Condensate (BEC). Plasma was identified in 1879 by William Crookes. The scientists working with Bose-Einstein Condensate received the Nobel Prize in 1995 for this work.

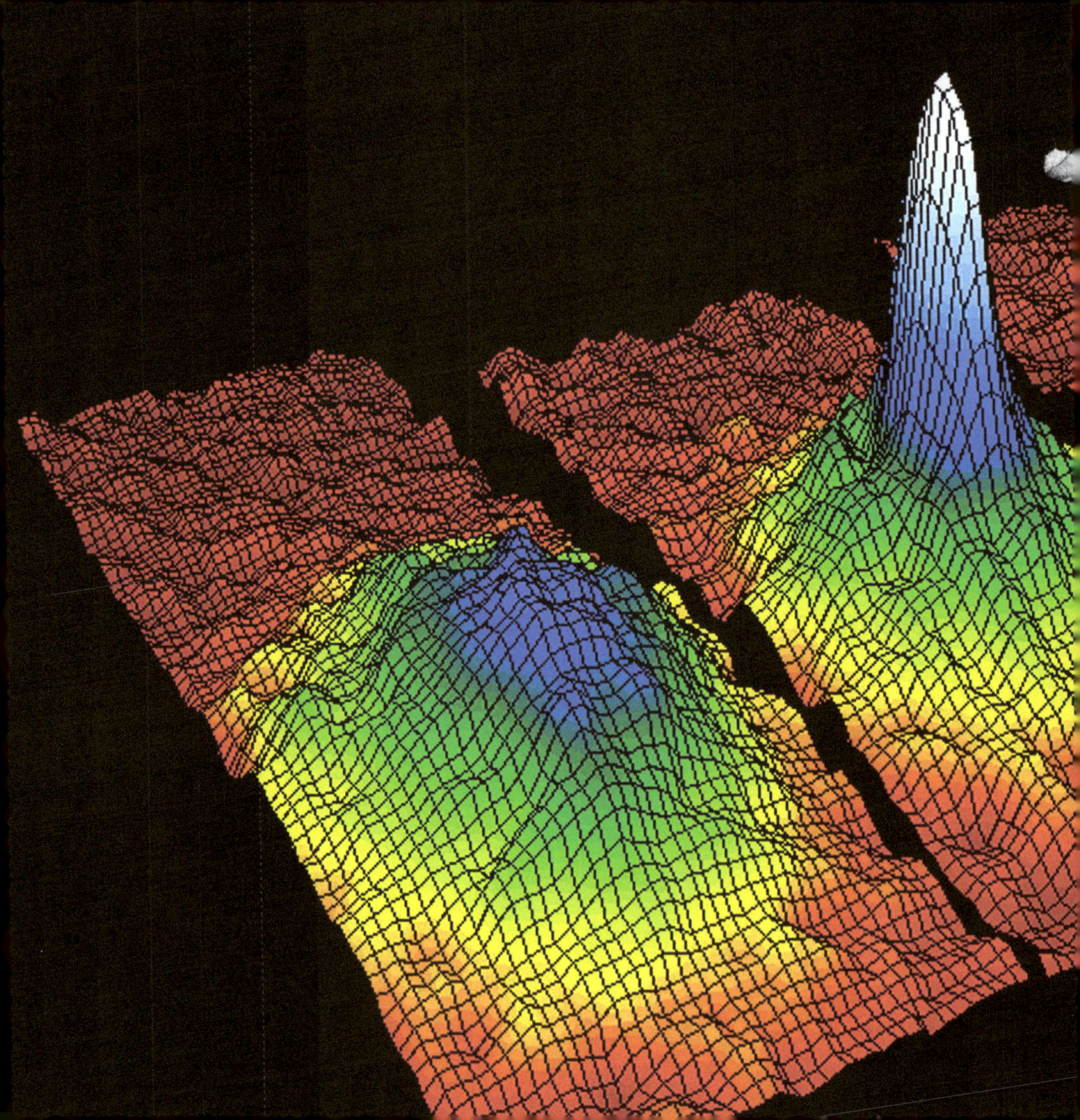

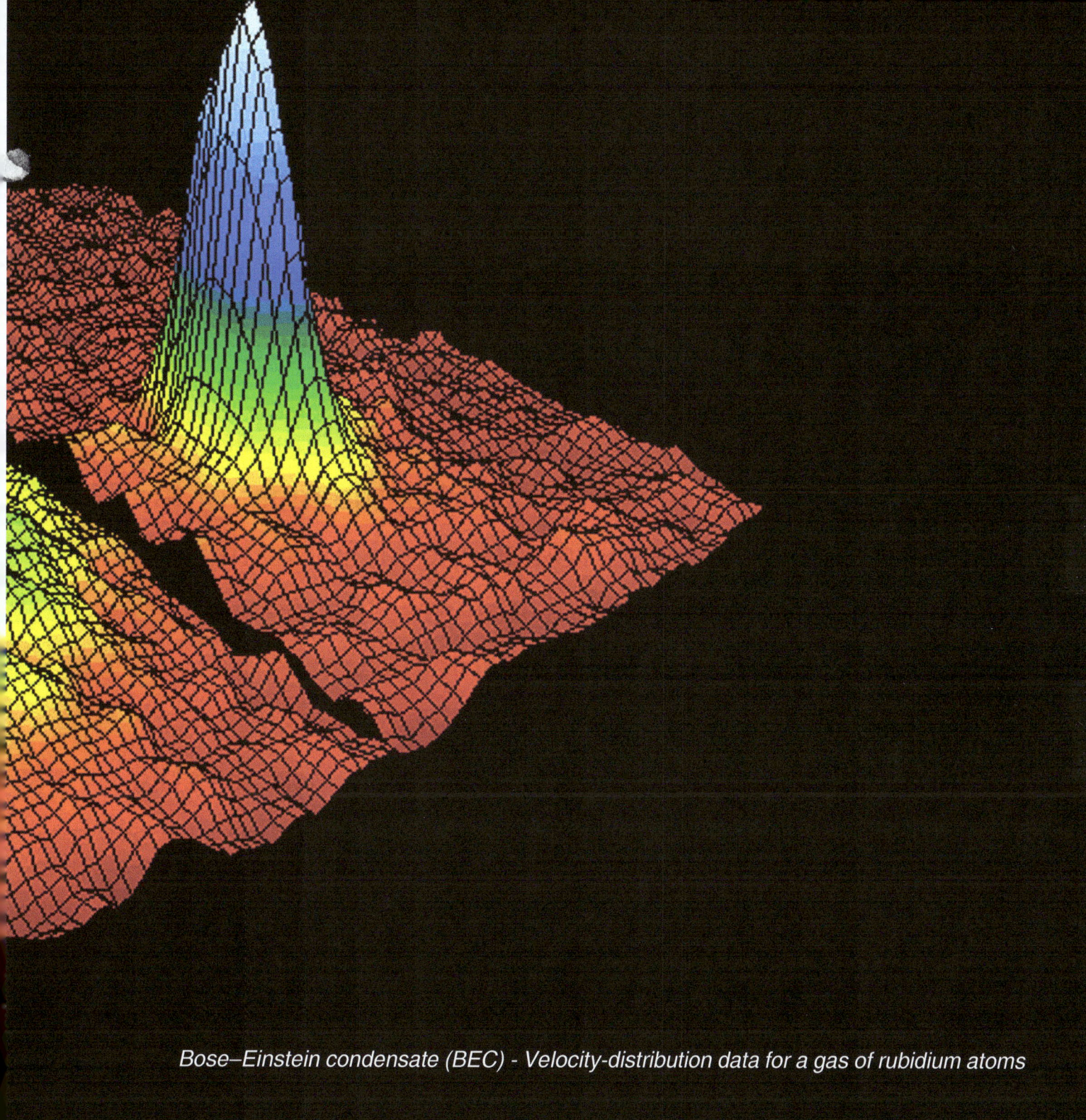

Bose–Einstein condensate (BEC) - Velocity-distribution data for a gas of rubidium atoms

WHAT MAKES A STATE OF MATTER?

It's all about the physical state of the atoms and the molecules. Solids are hard and brittle most of the time. On the other hand, liquids appear fluidic, moving around, and filling up containers. Gases always surround you, however the molecules of a gas are farther apart than those of a liquid. If a gas releases an odor, you will notice its smell before you are able to see it. The BEC is about the atoms and are less energetic and closer than the atoms of a liquid.

Liquids, solids, plasma, gases, and BEC are considered different states and they each have different physical properties. Each of these is known as a phase. Compounds and elements have the ability to move from phase to phase when changes occur in certain physical conditions. An example would be that as the temperature of a system rises, the matter in that system them becomes more active and excited. If there is enough energy placed within a system, a phase change can also occur once the matter changes to a more active state.

Sulphuric gas emerging from the volcanic crater

Think about a glass of water. As the temperature rises in the water, the molecules become more excited and start bouncing around more. If you provide the liquid water molecule with enough energy, it will escape the liquid phase and turn into a gas.

Have you noticed that as a turkey dinner heats up how wonderful it smells? The energy of the molecules in the turkey become warmer and escape as a gas. You are able to then smell the volatile molecules mixed within the air.

Ice sculpture

CHANGING STATES OF MATTER

While molecules and atoms do not change, the way they move around does change. As an example, water always consists of one oxygen atom and two hydrogen atoms. It can, however, change states into a *liquid*, a *solid (ice)*, or a *gas (steam)*. These changes take place as energy is added. This energy is often seen in the form of pressure or heat.

Water is a transparent and nearly colorless chemical substance that is the main constituent of Earth's streams, lakes, and oceans, and the fluid of most living organisms.

WATER

Water in its solid form is known as ice, which is water having the lowest temperature and energy. In this solid form, its molecules are tight and do not move easily. Water in its liquid form is water. One the temperature of ice increases, it changes to its liquid phase, liquid water.

Boiling water

These molecules are loose and can around more easily. Water in its gas form is known as vapor or steam. As water begins to boil, it turns into vapor. At this point, the molecules are looser, hotter, and able to move faster than liquid molecules. They are spread farther apart and can be squished or compressed.

Melting Ice Cubes

SOLID TO LIQUID AND THEN BACK TO SOLID

Imagine being a solid. You're an ice cube sitting on a table. You want to become liquid water. You need the help in the form of energy. Heat is more than likely the easiest form of energy to assist you in changing your physical state. The atoms contained in the liquid will have more than in the solid.

The melting point is the temperature that every substance reaches when it becomes a liquid. In the instance of water, that temperature is just over 0 degrees Celsius. Opposite of melting is known as freezing. Once water as a liquid freezes it becomes solid ice as its molecules lose their energy.

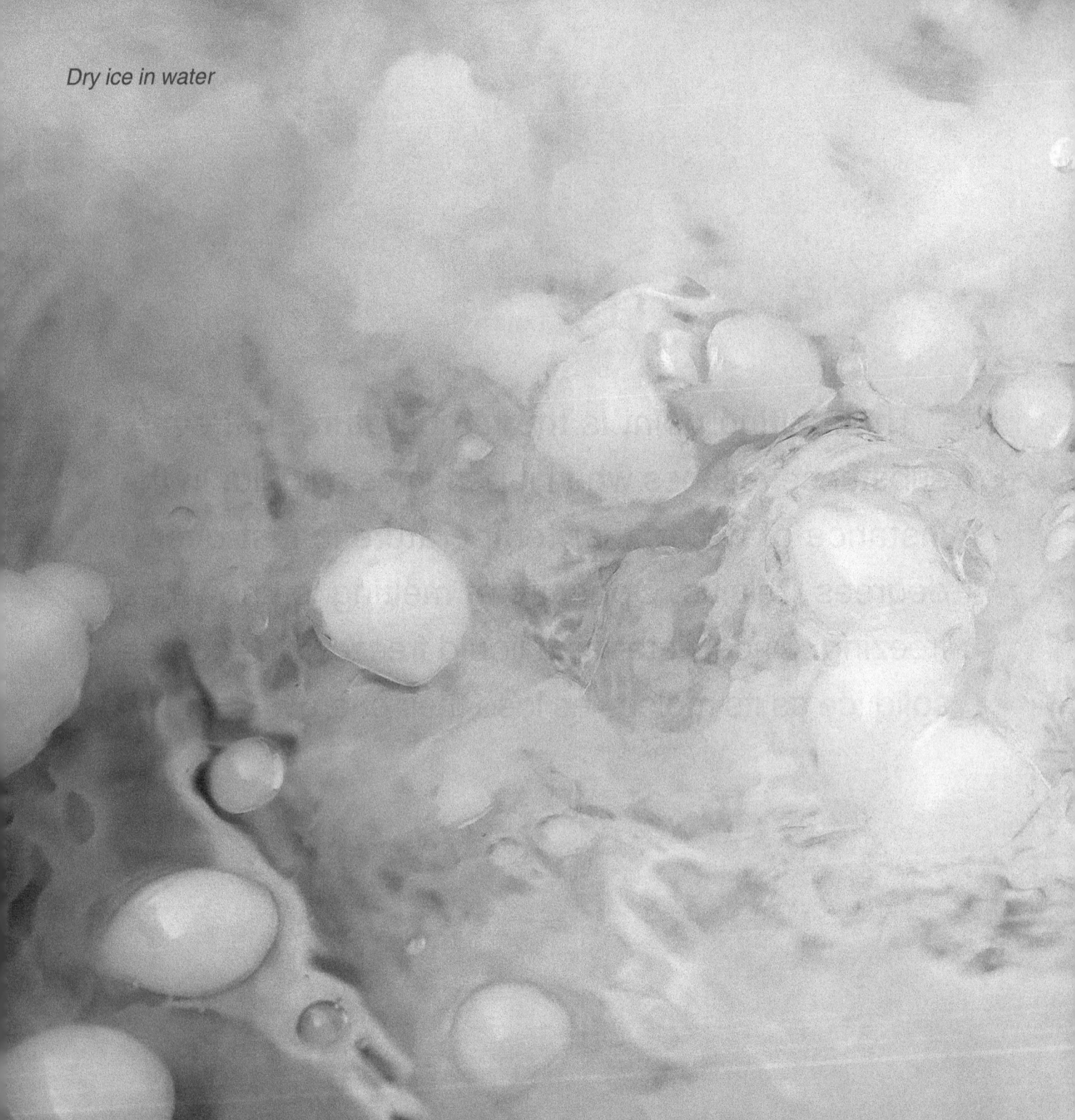
Dry ice in water

SOLID TO GAS AND THEN BACK TO SOLID

In the previous section, you learned about solids melting and turning into liquids. Sublimation is the process of a solid becoming a gas. Dry ice would be a good example of this. It is carbon dioxide in its solid form. When it is left out, it turns into a gas. Coal is also an example of something that does not melt at typical pressures. It takes extremely high temperatures for it to sublimate.

When a gas turns into a solid without traveling through a matter's liquid state, is known as deposition. If you live close to the equator you may not have seen this, but in colder climates, it is known as frost on those cold wintery mornings. The frost crystals that you see on plants occur as the water vapor turns to solid on the plant's leaves.

Molecules and atoms

THE ATOM

This is the basic of all matter. They are very small and consist of even tinier particles. Neutrons, protons, and electrons are the basic particles making up the atom. Atoms join together with other atoms and create matter. It takes many atoms to create anything. The human body is made up of so many that it is almost impossible to write the number down. Probably somewhere in the trillions.

Atom icon

The different atoms are created from the number of neutrons, protons, and electrons that is contained in each atom. Each different type of atom represents an element. There are 92 elements in their natural form, and up to 118 if you include the elements that are man-made. For the most part, they can last forever.

They have the ability to change and also undergo chemical reactions, by sharing electrons with the other atoms. The nucleus is difficult to split, which means that most of them hang around for a very long time.

STRUCTURE OF THE ATOM

The atom's center is known as the nucleus. It consists of neutrons and protons. Its electron's spin in orbits that surround the nucleus.

Atom Structure

ATOM STRUCTURE

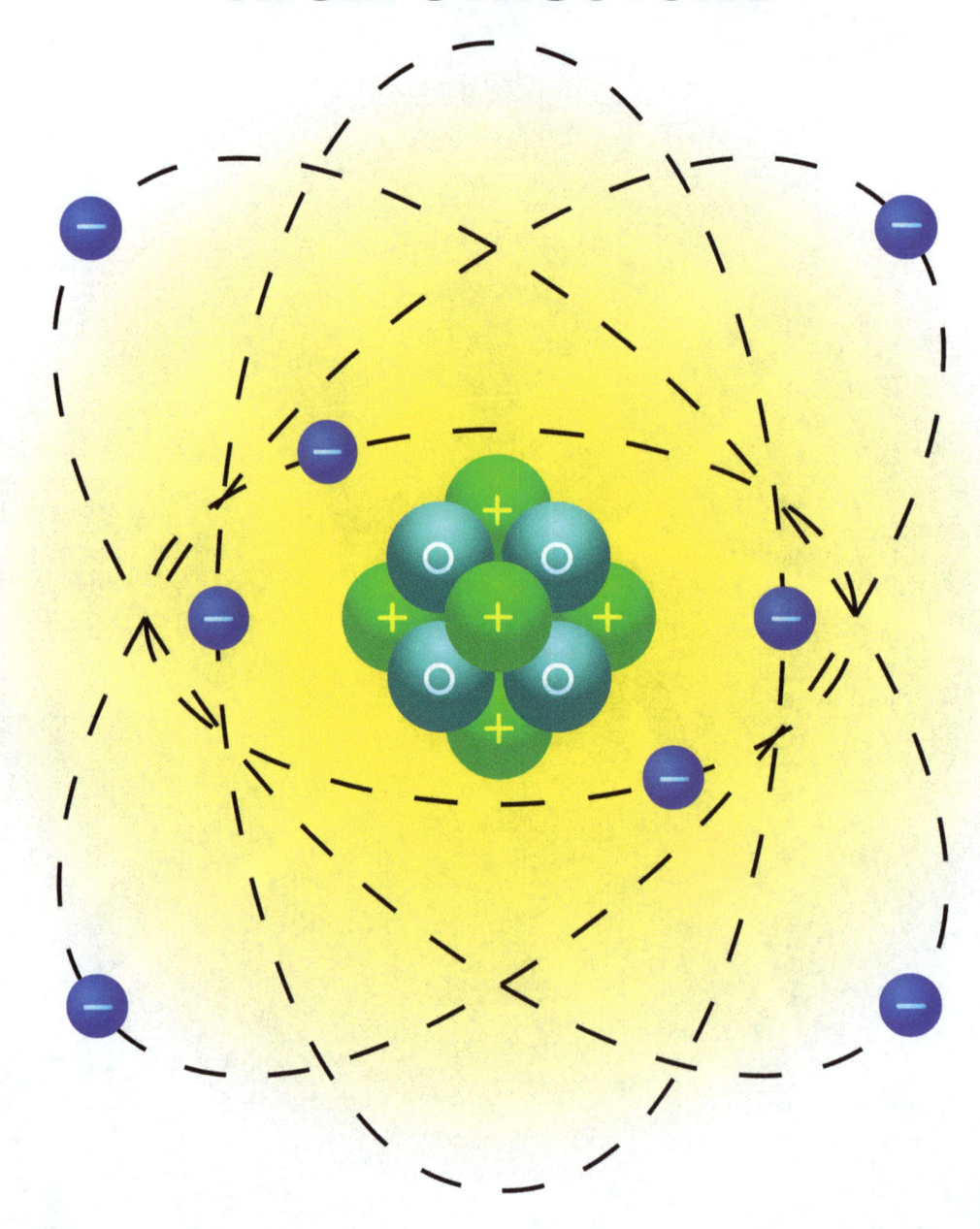

+ 🟢 Proton   ○ 🔵 Neutron   − 🔵 Electron

THE PROTON

The particle that is positively charged at the atom's center is known as the proton. The only atom that contains one proton and no neutron is hydrogen.

THE ELECTRON

The negatively charged particle that spins outside the nucleus is known as the electron. They spin so quickly around its nucleus that scientists cannot be 100% sure as to their location. If an atom contains the same number of protons and neutrons, it is considered to have a neutral charge. The electrons are pulled to the atom's nucleus by the positive charge provided by its protons. Electrons are smaller than protons and neutrons. Around 1800 times as small!

ATOM STRUCTURE

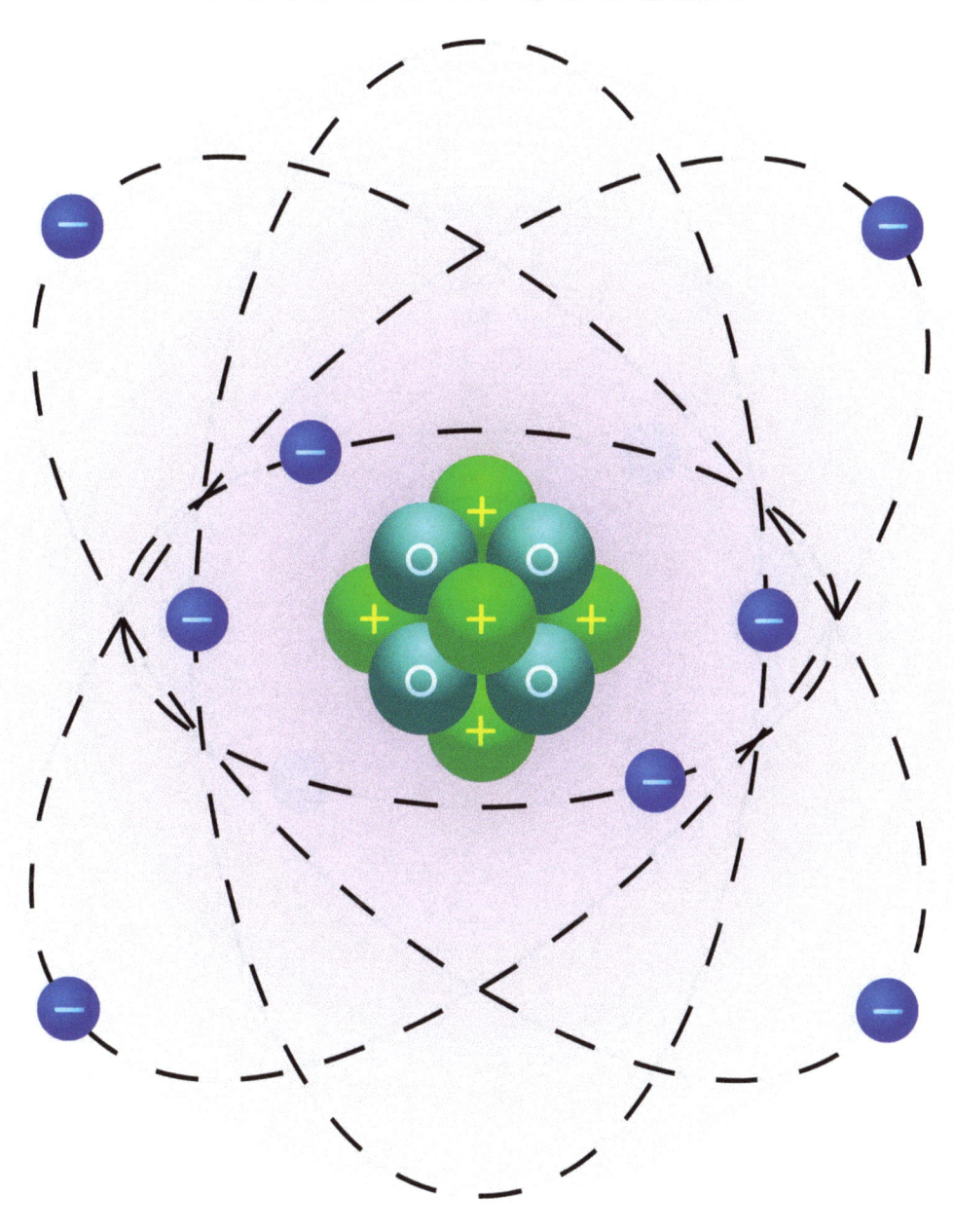

+ ● Proton   ○ ● Neutron   − ● Electron

ATOM STRUCTURE

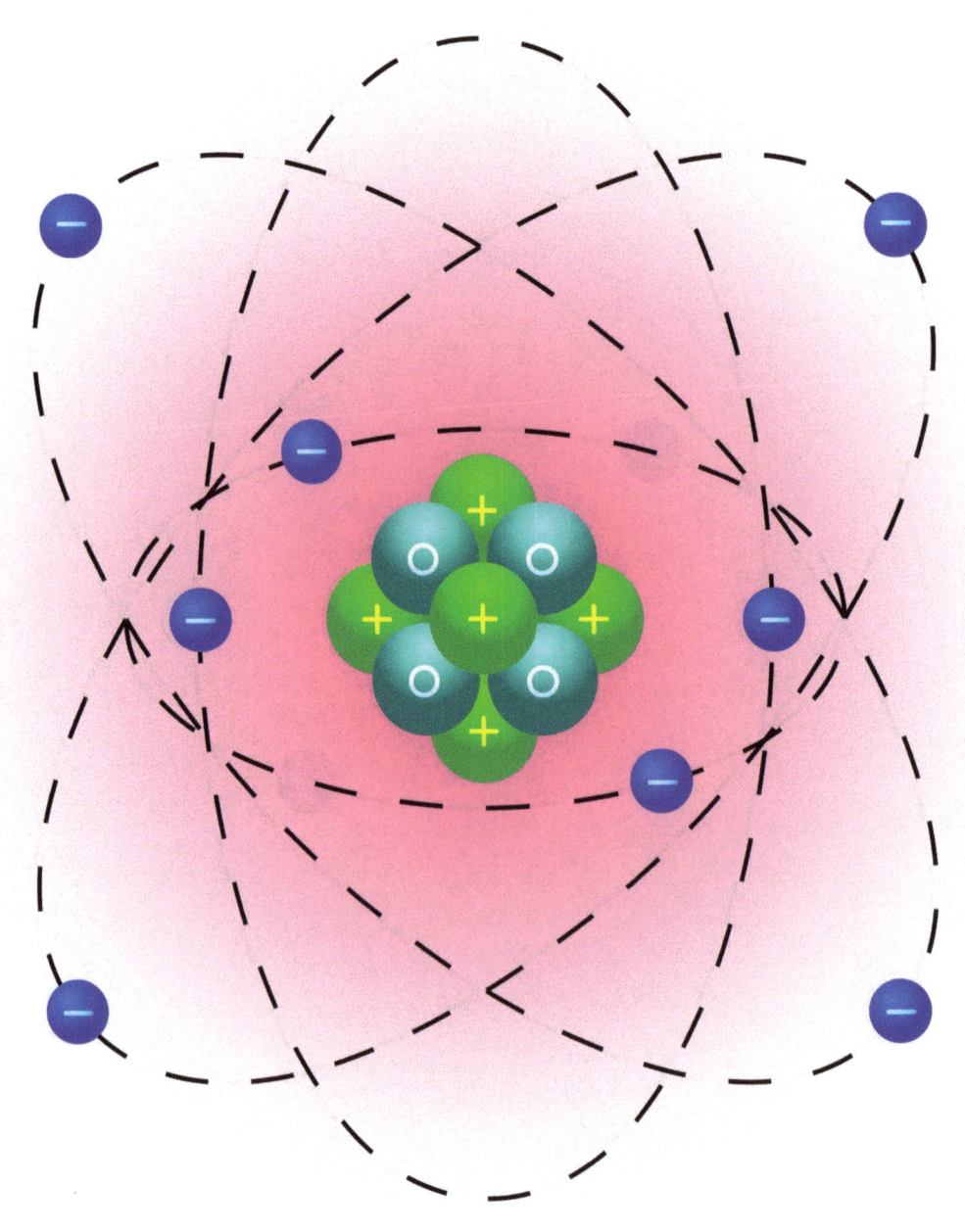

+ ● Proton   ○ ● Neutron   − ● Electron

THE NEUTRON

Particles in an atom having a neutral charge are known as neutrons. They are neither positive or negative. That does not mean that they do not play a major role in an atom. Each part of an atom is necessary for the atom to behave and act as it does. This includes the neutrons.

OTHER PARTICLES

QUARK – These are tiny particles that create the protons and neutrons. Quarks are almost impossible to notice and were only recently discovered, in 1964 by Murray Gell-Mann. There are six different types: top, bottom, up, down, strange, and charm.

Atom model with Quarks inside Proton and Neutron

STANDARD MODEL OF ELEMENTARY PARTICLES

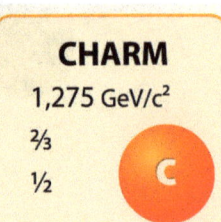

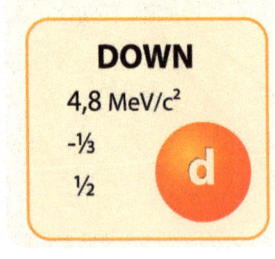

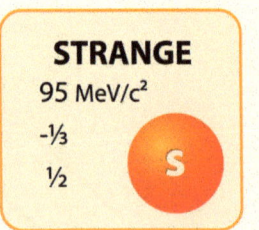

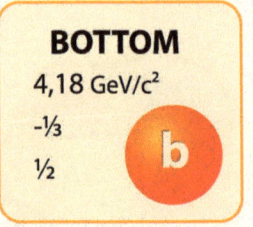

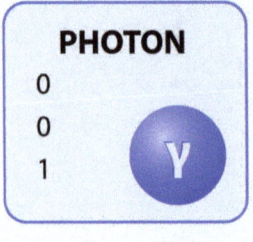

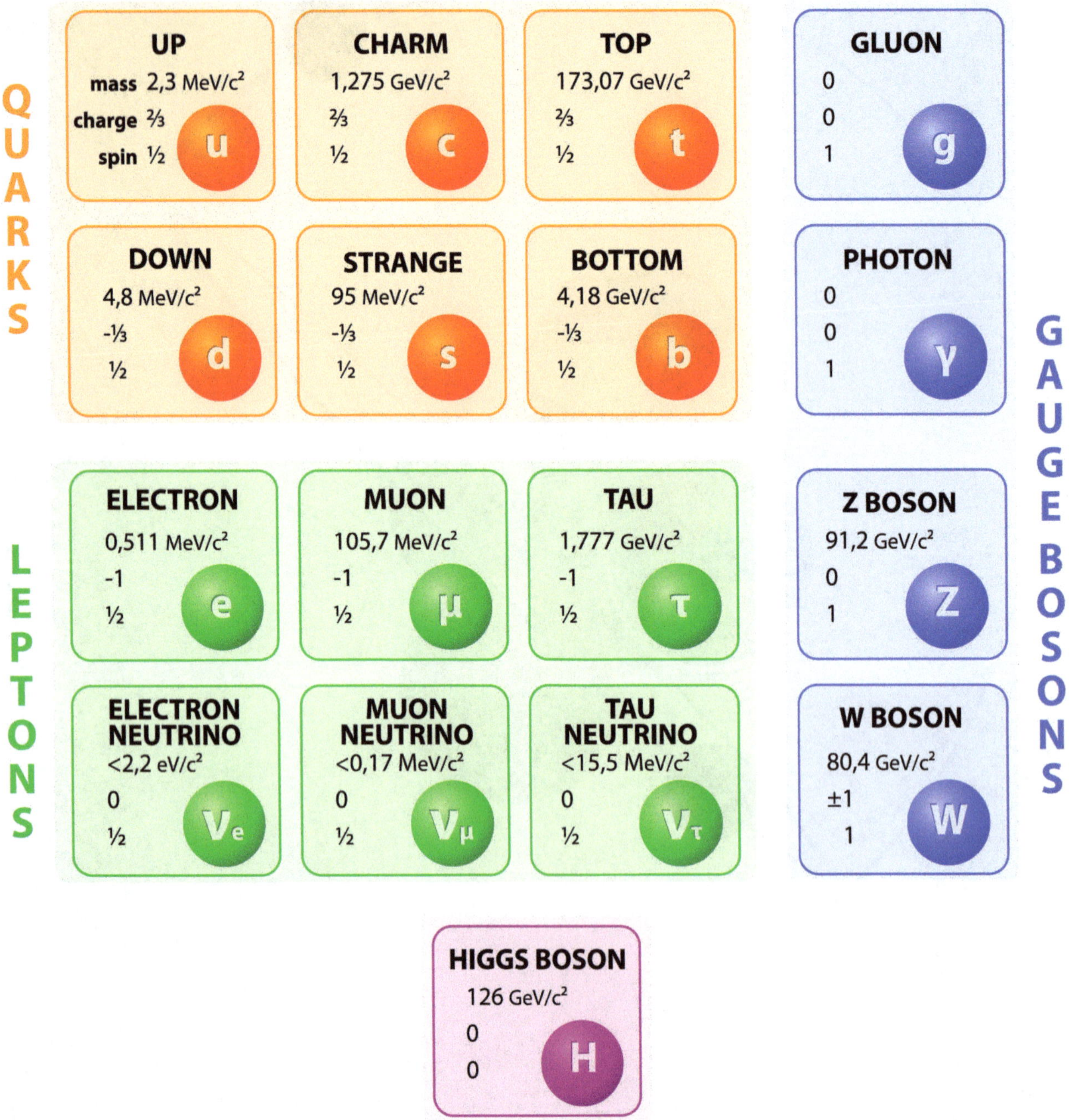

QUARKS

UP	CHARM	TOP
mass 2,3 MeV/c²	1,275 GeV/c²	173,07 GeV/c²
charge ⅔	⅔	⅔
spin ½	½	½
u	c	t

DOWN	STRANGE	BOTTOM
4,8 MeV/c²	95 MeV/c²	4,18 GeV/c²
-⅓	-⅓	-⅓
½	½	½
d	s	b

LEPTONS

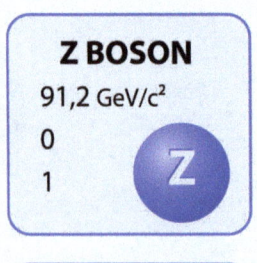

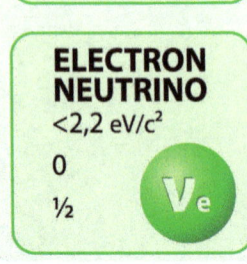

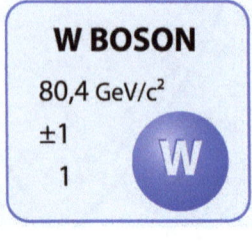

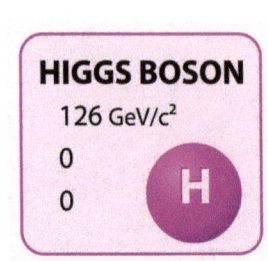

ELECTRON	MUON	TAU
0,511 MeV/c²	105,7 MeV/c²	1,777 GeV/c²
-1	-1	-1
½	½	½
e	μ	τ

ELECTRON NEUTRINO	MUON NEUTRINO	TAU NEUTRINO
<2,2 eV/c²	<0,17 MeV/c²	<15,5 MeV/c²
0	0	0
½	½	½
ν_e	ν_μ	ν_τ

GAUGE BOSONS

GLUON	PHOTON	Z BOSON	W BOSON
0	0	91,2 GeV/c²	80,4 GeV/c²
0	0	0	±1
1	1	1	1
g	γ	Z	W

HIGGS BOSON
126 GeV/c²
0
0
H

NEUTRINO – Nuclear reactions create neutrinos. They are similar to electrons that don't have a charge and usually they travel at the speed of light. The sun emits more than a trillion of neutrinos each second. They have the ability to pass through a solid object, including the human body.

MOLECULES

When two atoms join, they create a molecule. Everything around consists of molecules, including the human body. The human body actually consists of trillions of various types of molecules.

MOLECULE

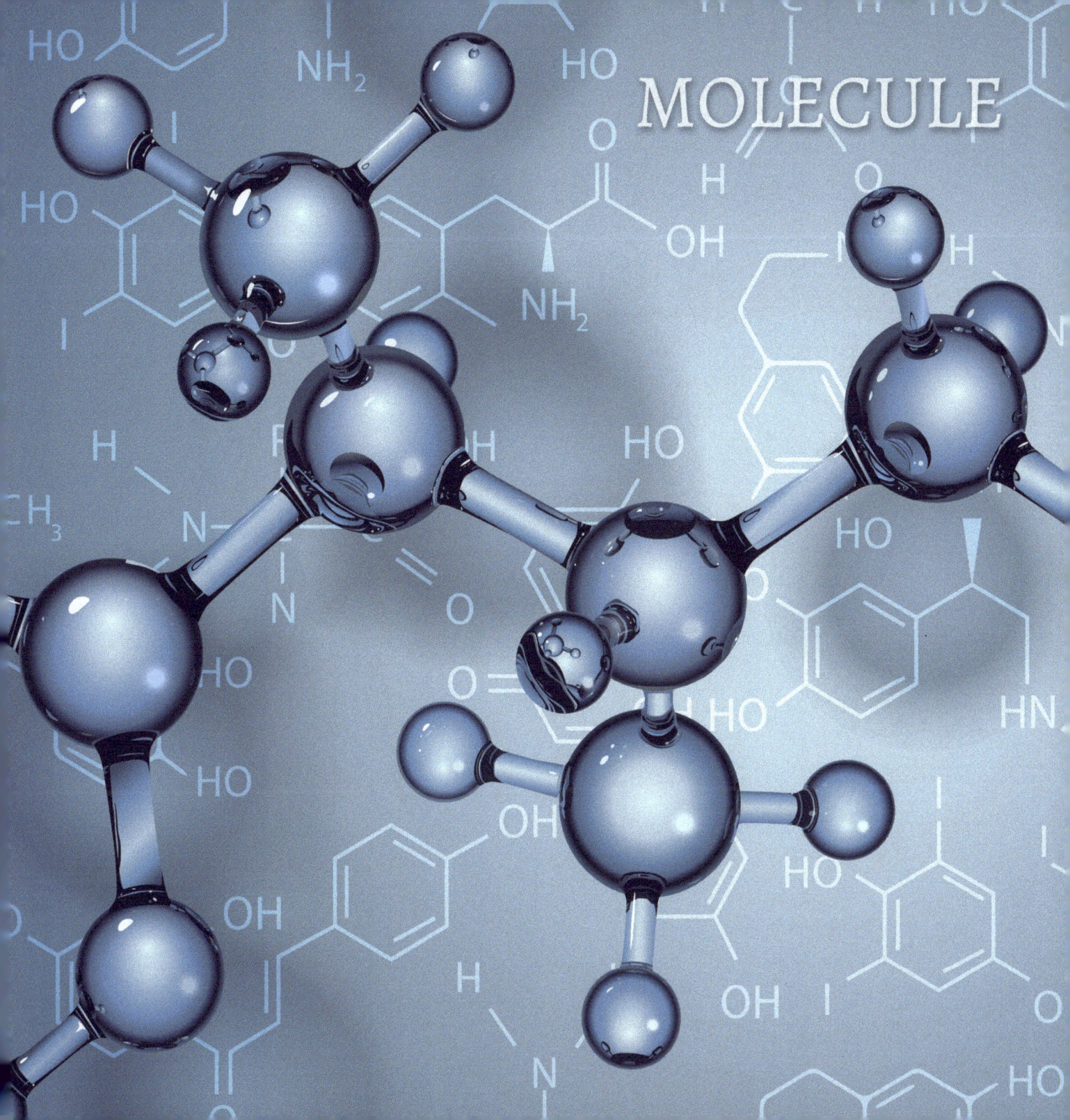

Water - H_2O

COMPOUNDS

When atoms of different types join, they create molecules known as compounds. Water is made of compound molecules consisting of 2 hydrogen and 1 oxygen atoms. That is why it is referred to as H_2O. Water will always consist of two times the amount of hydrogen atoms as its oxygen atoms.

HOW ARE COMPOUNDS NAMED?

Chemists follow specific rules in naming compounds, and scientists all over the world follow these same standards when naming a compound. A compounds name is structured from its elements and molecular construction.

MOLECULAR STRUCTURE

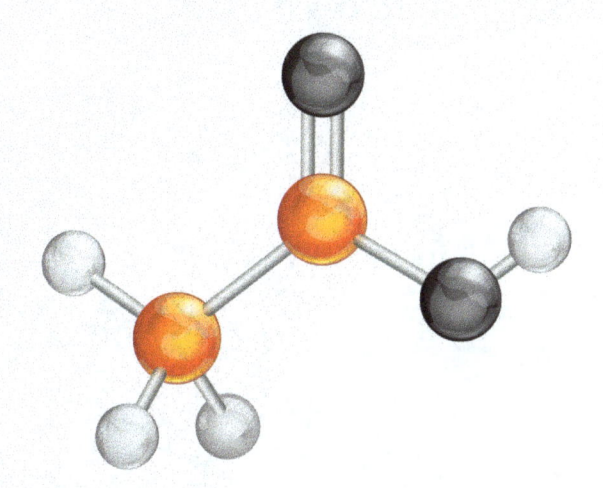

Acetic acid CH_3COOH

Methane CH_4

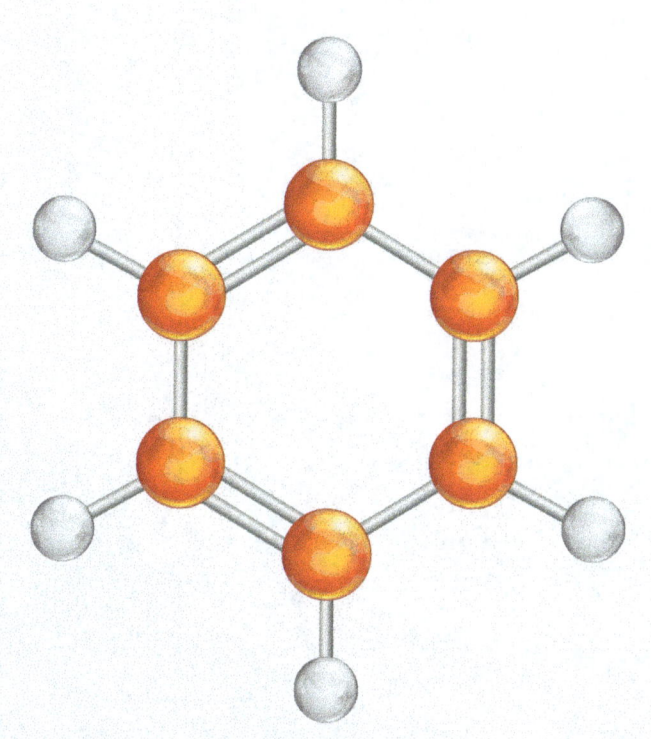

Water H_2O

Benzene C_6H_6

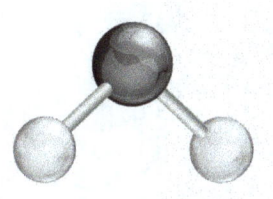

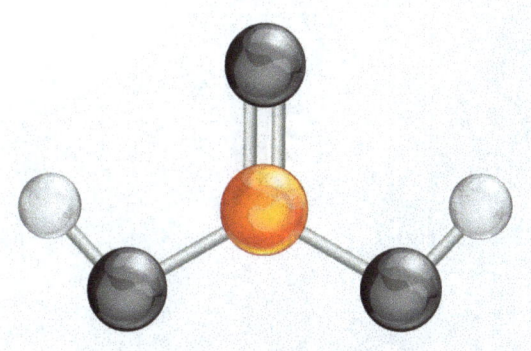

Carbonic acid H_2CO_3

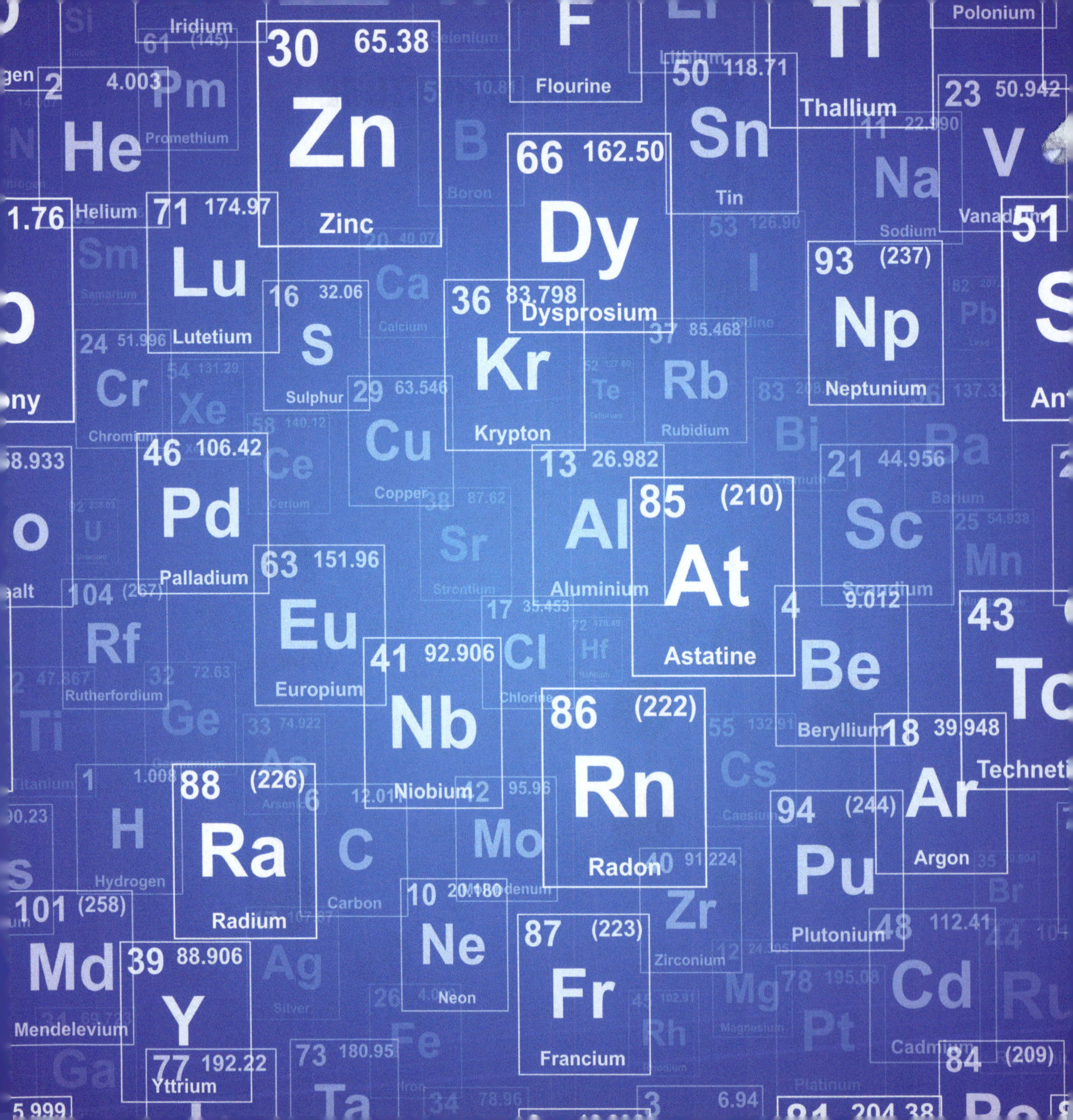

30 65.38 Zn Zinc
2 4.003 He Helium
71 174.97 Lu Lutetium
66 162.50 Dy Dysprosium
Flourine
50 118.71 Sn Tin
Thallium
23 50.942 V
93 (237) Np Neptunium
16 32.06 S Sulphur
36 83.798 Kr Krypton
46 106.42 Pd Palladium
13 26.982 Al Aluminium
85 (210) At Astatine
21 44.956 Sc Scandium
63 151.96 Eu Europium
41 92.906 Nb Niobium
4 9.012 Be Beryllium
43 Tc
86 (222) Rn Radon
18 39.948 Ar Argon
88 (226) Ra Radium
94 (244) Pu Plutonium
10 20.180 Ne Neon
87 (223) Fr Francium
39 88.906 Y Yttrium
101 (258) Md Mendelevium
104 (267) Rf Rutherfordium
48 112.41 Cd Cadmium
84 (209)

THE PERIODIC TABLE OF ELEMENTS

The Periodic Table is how the elements are listed. The elements are listed by their atomic structure, which includes the number of protons and the number of electrons contained in their outer shell. They are listed left to right and top to bottom in order by their atomic number, the number of protons contained in each atom.

PERIODIC TABLE OF THE ELEMENTS

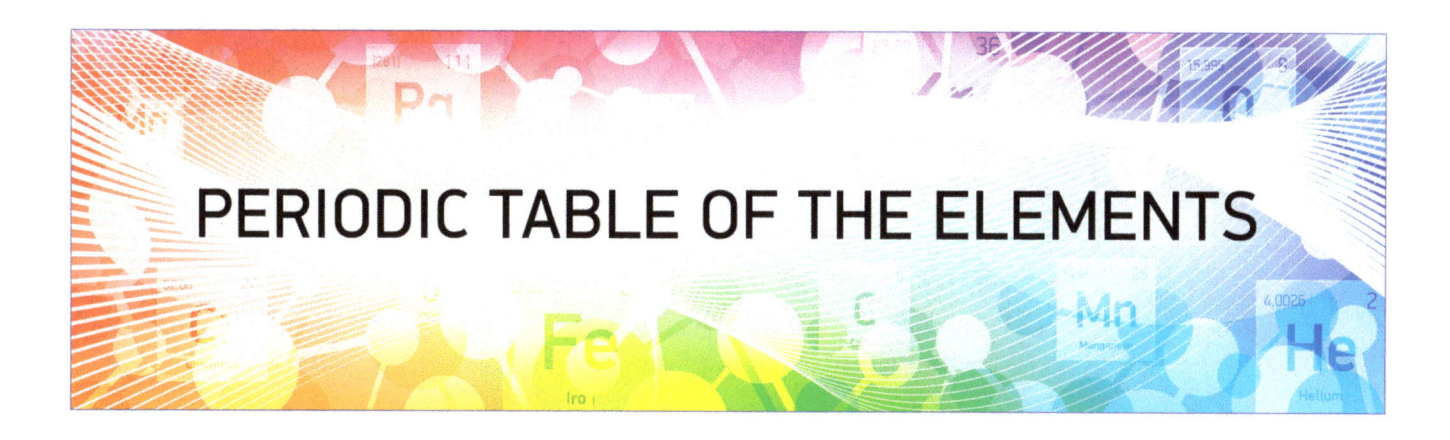

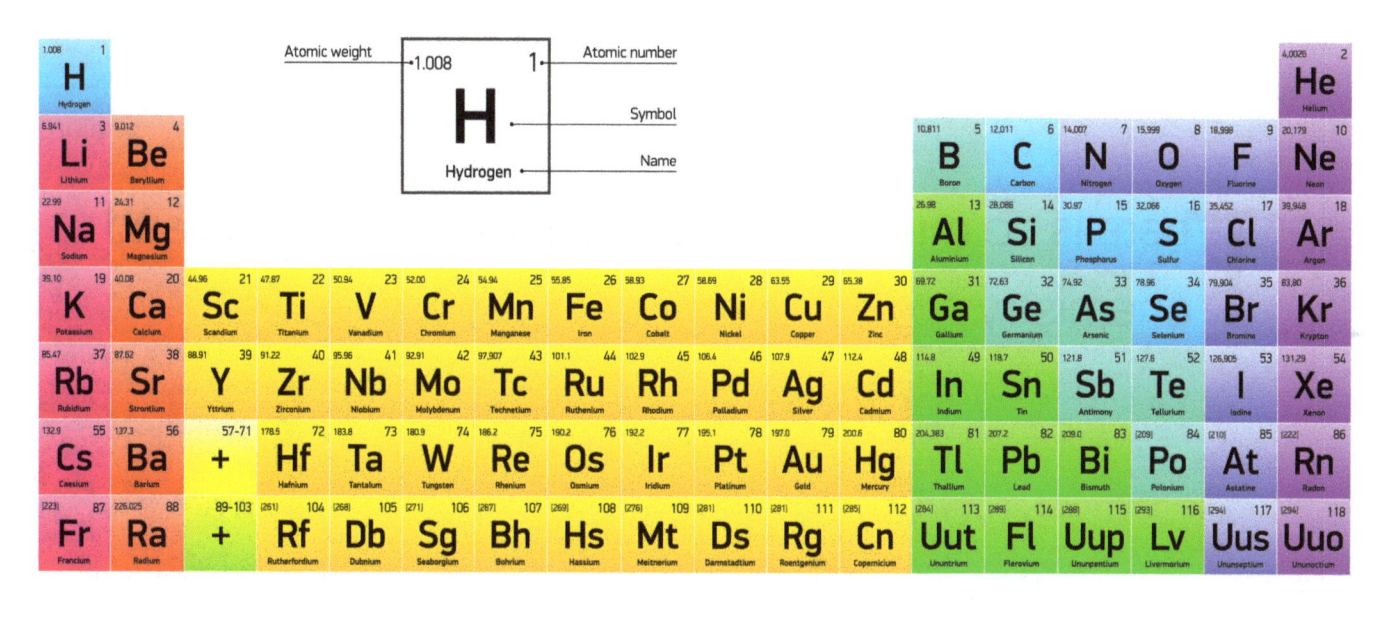

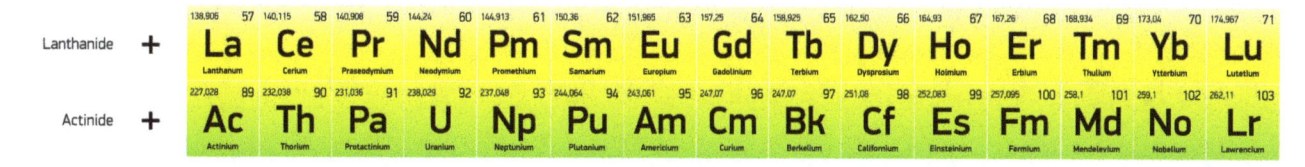

1.008 1 H Hydrogen																	4.0026 2 He Helium
6.941 3 Li Lithium	9.012 4 Be Beryllium											10.811 5 B Boron	12.011 6 C Carbon	14.007 7 N Nitrogen	15.999 8 O Oxygen	18.998 9 F Fluorine	20.179 10 Ne Neon
22.99 11 Na Sodium	24.31 12 Mg Magnesium											26.98 13 Al Aluminium	28.086 14 Si Silicon	30.97 15 P Phosphorus	32.066 16 S Sulfur	35.452 17 Cl Chlorine	39.948 18 Ar Argon
39.10 19 K Potassium	40.08 20 Ca Calcium	44.96 21 Sc Scandium	47.87 22 Ti Titanium	50.94 23 V Vanadium	52.00 24 Cr Chromium	54.94 25 Mn Manganese	55.85 26 Fe Iron	58.93 27 Co Cobalt	58.69 28 Ni Nickel	63.55 29 Cu Copper	65.38 30 Zn Zinc	69.72 31 Ga Gallium	72.63 32 Ge Germanium	74.92 33 As Arsenic	78.96 34 Se Selenium	79.904 35 Br Bromine	83.80 36 Kr Krypton
85.47 37 Rb Rubidium	87.62 38 Sr Strontium	88.91 39 Y Yttrium	91.22 40 Zr Zirconium	92.91 41 Nb Niobium	95.96 42 Mo Molybdenum	97.907 43 Tc Technetium	101.1 44 Ru Ruthenium	102.9 45 Rh Rhodium	106.4 46 Pd Palladium	107.9 47 Ag Silver	112.4 48 Cd Cadmium	114.8 49 In Indium	118.7 50 Sn Tin	121.8 51 Sb Antimony	127.6 52 Te Tellurium	126.905 53 I Iodine	131.29 54 Xe Xenon
132.9 55 Cs Caesium	137.3 56 Ba Barium	57-71 +	178.5 72 Hf Hafnium	183.8 73 Ta Tantalum	180.9 74 W Tungsten	186.2 75 Re Rhenium	190.2 76 Os Osmium	192.2 77 Ir Iridium	195.1 78 Pt Platinum	197.0 79 Au Gold	200.6 80 Hg Mercury	204.383 81 Tl Thallium	207.2 82 Pb Lead	209.0 83 Bi Bismuth	[209] 84 Po Polonium	[210] 85 At Astatine	[222] 86 Rn Radon
[223] 87 Fr Francium	226.025 88 Ra Radium	89-103 +	[261] 104 Rf Rutherfordium	[268] 105 Db Dubnium	[271] 106 Sg Seaborgium	[267] 107 Bh Bohrium	[269] 108 Hs Hassium	[276] 109 Mt Meitnerium	[281] 110 Ds Darmstadtium	[281] 111 Rg Roentgenium	[285] 112 Cn Copernicium	[284] 113 Uut Ununtrium	[289] 114 Fl Flerovium	[288] 115 Uup Ununpentium	[293] 116 Lv Livermorium	[294] 117 Uus Ununseptium	[294] 118 Uuo Ununoctium

Atomic weight → 1.008 1 ← **Atomic number**
H ← **Symbol**
Hydrogen ← **Name**

Lanthanide +

138.906 57 La Lanthanum	140.115 58 Ce Cerium	140.908 59 Pr Praseodymium	144.24 60 Nd Neodymium	144.913 61 Pm Promethium	150.36 62 Sm Samarium	151.965 63 Eu Europium	157.25 64 Gd Gadolinium	158.925 65 Tb Terbium	162.50 66 Dy Dysprosium	164.93 67 Ho Holmium	167.26 68 Er Erbium	168.934 69 Tm Thulium	173.04 70 Yb Ytterbium	174.967 71 Lu Lutetium

Actinide +

227.028 89 Ac Actinium	232.038 90 Th Thorium	231.036 91 Pa Protactinium	238.029 92 U Uranium	237.048 93 Np Neptunium	244.064 94 Pu Plutonium	243.061 95 Am Americium	247.07 96 Cm Curium	247.07 97 Bk Berkelium	251.08 98 Cf Californium	252.083 99 Es Einsteinium	257.095 100 Fm Fermium	258.1 101 Md Mendelevium	259.1 102 No Nobelium	262.11 103 Lr Lawrencium

- Alkali metal
- Alkaline earth metal
- Transition metal
- Post-transition metal
- Metalloid
- Polyatomic nonmetal
- Diatomic nonmetal
- Noble gas

There is so much more to learn about solutions and chemistry.

For additional information on Chemical Solutions, you can research the internet, go to your local library, and ask questions of your teachers, family, and friends.

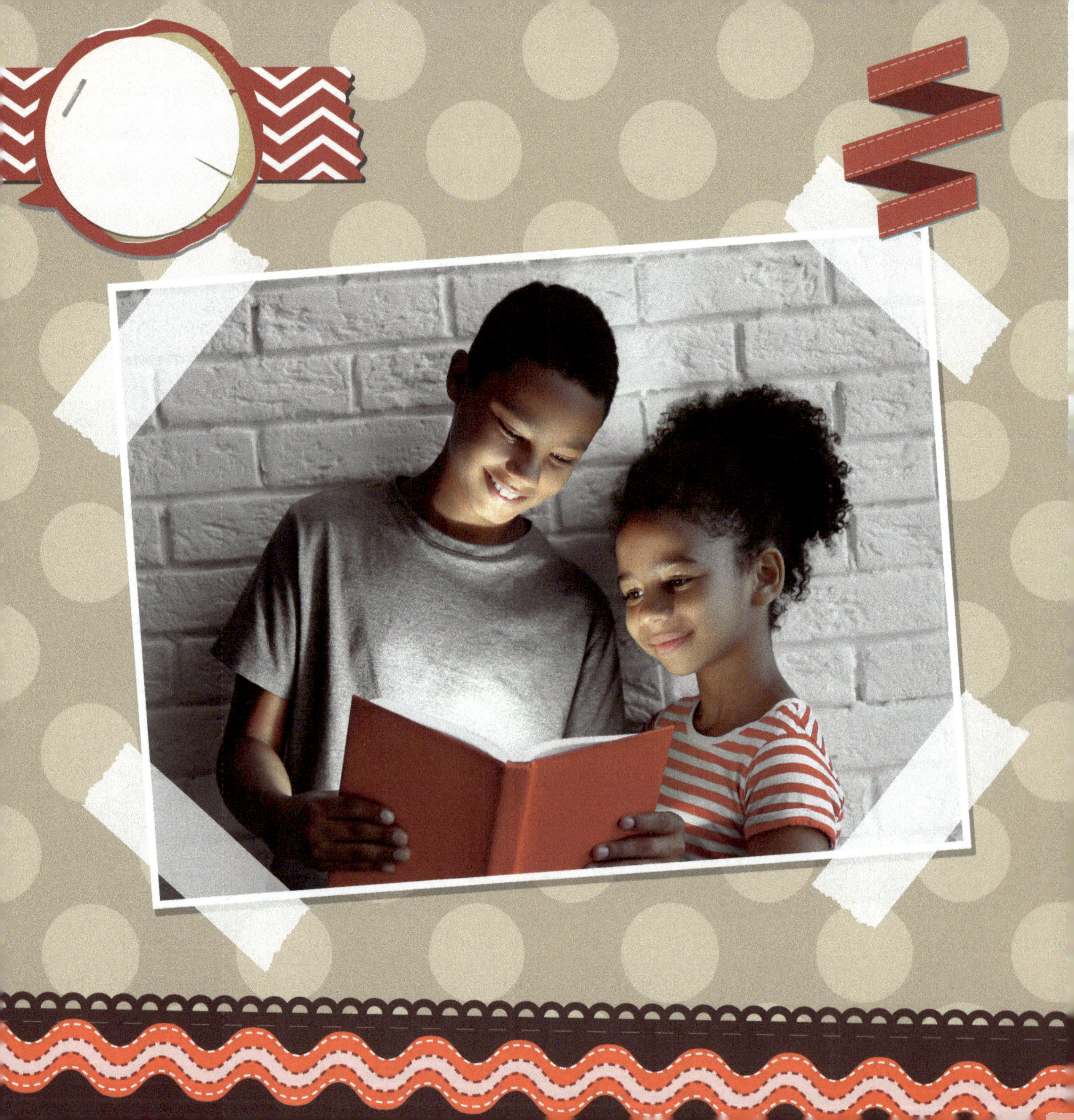

Visit

BABY PROFESSOR
EDUCATION KIDS

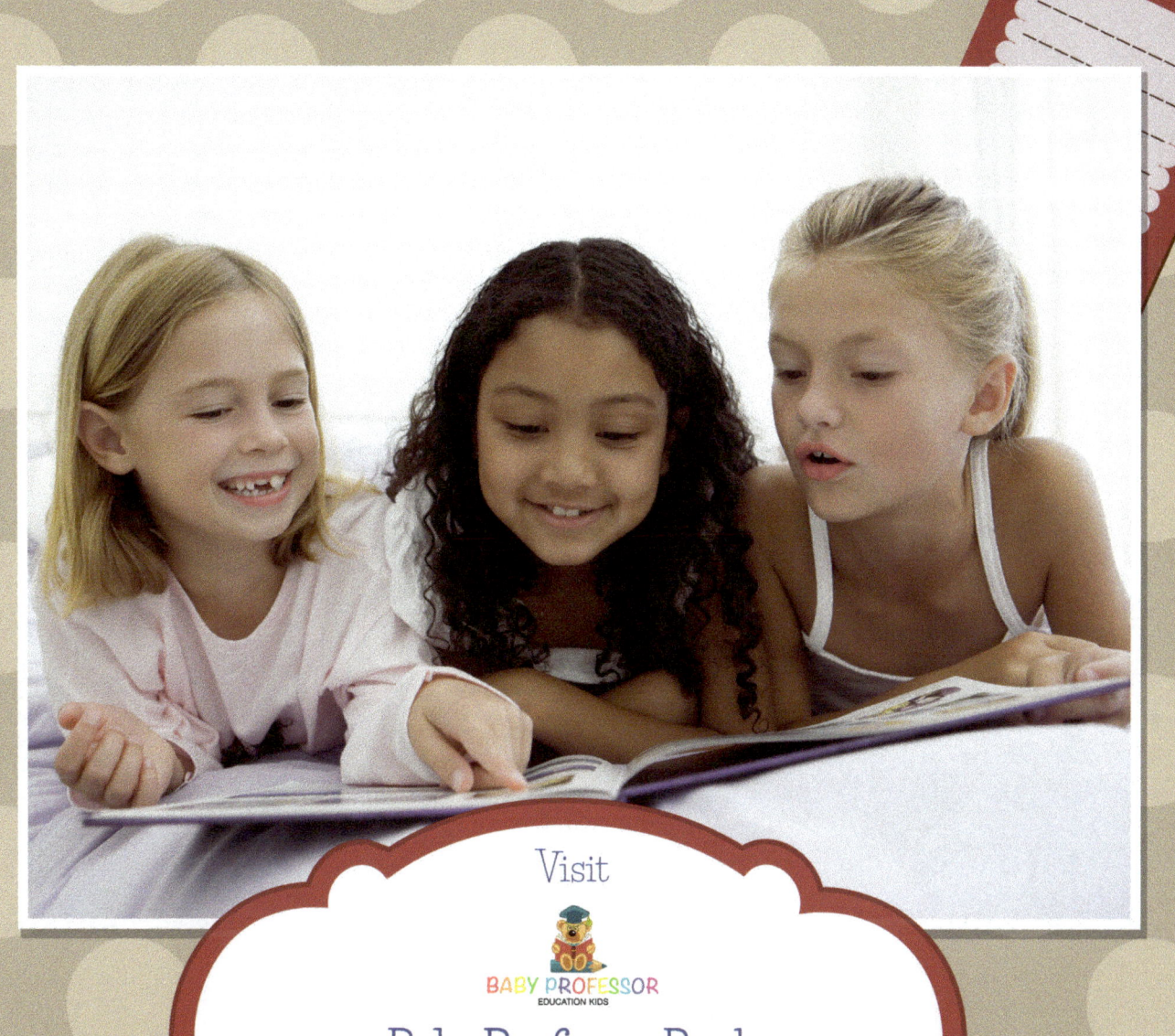

www.BabyProfessorBooks.com

to download Free Baby Professor eBooks and view our catalog of new and exciting Children's Books

Milton Keynes UK
Ingram Content Group UK Ltd.
UKHW051143030924
447802UK00003B/317

9 798869 410528